INDIA

INDIA

JOHN L. STODDARD

GYAN

Published by

Gyan Publishing House
5, Ansari Road
Daryaganj, New Delhi-110002
Phone: 011-47034999, 9811692060
E-mail: books@gyanbooks.com

Distribution Network
gyanbooks.com
India, USA, Canada, UK, Australia, France

ISBN: 978-81-212-8752-4 (PB)
First Published, 1897

2nd Impression 2023

Printed at: Gyan Press, Delhi.

INDIA
Author: John L. Stoddard

INDIA

BY

JOHN L. STODDARD

ILLUSTRATED AND EMBELLISHED WITH ONE HUNDRED AND TWELVE REPRODUCTIONS OF PHOTOGRAPHS

CHICAGO
BELFORD, MIDDLEBROOK & COMPANY
MDCCCXCVII

INDIA

INDIA is in some respects the most difficult country in the world to understand. One thinks of it at times as one great nation, governed, it is true, by England, but still constituting one homogeneous people. Nothing is further from the truth. It is a vast conglomeration of principalities and races, in some instances as different from each other as is France from Germany. The natives do not even speak a common tongue. There are in India no less than two hundred distinct dialects, each unintelligible to speakers of any of the others; while, as if this were not enough, the people of the same community are subdivided into castes which will not even eat with one another. And how appalling is their number — three hundred millions, — nearly one-fifth of the entire race, and

A MOHAMMEDAN.

double the population of the Roman Empire when its extent was greatest! The amount of territory occupied by these millions is enormous. The province of Lower Bengal is as large as France; that of Madras exceeds Great Britain and Ireland; that of Bombay equals Germany in area; and the size of the Punjab rivals that of Italy.

To comprehend the heterogeneous mass inhabiting India appears at first as difficult as to explore an Indian jungle; but

THE HUGLI RIVER.

there is one trusty clue to guide us through the labyrinth,—Religion. This will explain to us the customs of that land as nothing else can; for all these millions are so superstitious and fanatical that feelings of incredible intensity control their conduct from the cradle to the grave. After Hinduism, the second great religion which prevails in India is Mohammedanism. Nineteen out of every twenty people in India are either Hindus or Mohammedans. Victoria, Empress of India, has more Moslem subjects than the Sultan himself. There are no less than fifty-seven millions of them, or more than the entire Japanese nation. Their wealth and power, it is true, have

peared; but in the places where the Moslem ached the zenith of its glory their splendid archi- remains rival in elegance and grace the finest forms of ic or of Grecian art, and in themselves repay a journey around the world.

The gateway to India on its eastern coast is Calcutta, the rival of Bombay. As we approached it, the multitude of ships and steamers on the river Hugli exceeded anything that I had ever seen. For several miles we sailed past vessels of the largest size, frequently anchored five abreast. I was informed that one of these ships had just brought from England a hundred and twenty tons of gin and forty tons of Bibles. If this proportion is maintained on all of them, we may discover why the advent here of Christian nations is not regarded by the natives as an unmixed blessing. It is, however, probable that the gin is chiefly intended for the Europeans, while the poor heathen have to take the Bibles.

Unlike most Indian cities, Calcutta offers very little of historic interest. Two hundred years ago it was a cluster of mud huts. To-day, by reason of some handsome structures, such as its Post-office, it is proudly called the "City of Pal-

A NATIVE PALACE.

aces." Unfortunately, however, hovels are st
ous that I believe no other town in India reve
immedia
trast the
extremes of British wealth and native degradation. In what may be called Anglicized Calcutta are broad streets lined with statues and imposing buildings. The latter, being constructed of brick covered with painted stucco, are as a rule inferior to the public edifices of Bombay which are built of stone; nevertheless their size often renders them quite palatial in appearance.

ON THE MAIDAN.

The favorite promenade of Calcutta, known as Maidan, extends for more than two miles on the river-bank, and is as level as a parlor floor. Broad carriage-roads wind over it between expanses of soft turf and through a multitude of tropical plants. During the day its famous

ANGLICIZED CALCUTTA.

driveways are almost deserted. For while the sun retains it in his fiery grasp all Europeans shun it like a heated oven.

A CALCUTTA STREET.

Occasional statues of distinguished Englishmen then seem to be its only occupants. But when the solar shafts fall on this promenade obliquely, and pierce with difficulty, if at all, the drooping fringes of the palms, the British colony appears as if by magic, invading the vast area from all directions, much as the chorus of an opera troupe pours in upon an empty stage. Between five and seven o'clock the spectacle here displayed is rarely, if ever, equaled in the world. While military music stirs the balmy air, one sees along these avenues the most astonishing varieties of costumes and complexions. Even the simplest carriage of an English family will have its native coachman robed in white from head to foot and a dark groom resplendent in huge colored

A CALCUTTA "HERDIC."

turban and gold-embroidered jacket; and these, with Indian princes, wealthy Parsees, and rich Hindus, give to the scene a touch of Oriental splendor.

But, while the English in India are prudent enough to avoid the parks in the middle of the day, they have decided, absurdly enough, that the fashionable time for making calls shall be from twelve to two. One wretched victim of this social tyranny recently defined these Indian morning-calls as

> "The destruction that wasteth at noonday."

DRESSED FOR WORK.

We could not wonder that the English who reside in India look on Calcutta in the winter as an Eastern Paradise. It is, indeed, the centre of the Government, and here the Governor-general of India holds a court, said to surpass in brilliancy that of most European sovereigns. At Christmas time, especially, the town is thronged with officers of the army and navy and all the notable men in England's Indian service.

Then, also, hundreds of visitors from Europe, America, and Australia constitute a most distinguished and enjoyable society. But this is only one side of Calcutta. The native side is very different. The former is, of course, more agreeable to the English, and is the one more frequently described by travelers. But we all know what Europeans are like. The question is, what do the natives resemble? For, in India, where the foreigners number about one hundred thousand, the natives reach a population of three hundred millions. They are very easily studied at Calcutta, for at almost any point a short walk brings one from public buildings and spacious thoroughfares to the disgusting filth and poverty of the common Hindus. Most of the native streets are dirty alleys; most of their dwellings, hovels made of sun-dried mud or of bamboo poles covered with coarse matting. The occupants, in many instances, have their well-nigh naked bodies greased with rancid butter (which they consume internally as well), and even their hair is smeared with the same mixture. The pungent odor of this lubricant, combined with the smoke of burned manure, which is the fuel of India, gave to the atmosphere a peculiar quality which I shall always associate with Hindustan.

Some of the natives—tailors and cobblers—we found hard at work, seated in holes in a plastered wall, like dogs in their kennels. Even the splendor of the Mogul palaces which we afterward beheld could not make me forget this misery and degradation. India is a land of terrible extremes. Whatever is good there is superlatively good, and what is bad can hardly be imagined worse. Thus, in the matter of hotels, the very best in Calcutta is the Great Eastern; but it is my deliberate conviction, based upon an experience of many never-to-be-forgotten

THE NATIVE QUARTER.

days and nights, that, whereas, all the hotels in India are bad, those of Calcutta are worse than those of any city of its size and prominence in any country of the civilized world. It is true, the Great Eastern is well situated, and covers a great area; but in this case, "O, what a goodly outside falsehood hath!"

My traveling companion and myself, having telegraphed in advance, were assigned to a room on the best floor of the hotel. We reached it by a long, dark corridor about four feet wide. This space was made still smaller by a line of Hindu servants who were lying on the floor — one in front of each door. Through these we picked our way to room number "54." I give the number, not that the reader may specially avoid it when he goes there (since most of the other rooms are equally bad), but that, on seeing it, he may remember me and murmur: "There was a man who told the truth." The walls of this room did not come within two feet of the ceiling, and, as most of the other apartments were equally well ventilated, we assisted by day at half a dozen family quarrels, and at night could hear the whole brigade of Hindus snoring in the corridor. The Oriental way of calling servants is by clapping the hands. This is occasionally inconvenient; for in a room next to mine was a refractory

LIKE DOGS IN THEIR KENNELS.

THE TAJ MAHAL FROM THE RIVER.

child, and every time his mother spanked him all the servants in the entry responded to the call.

Number "54" was a whitewashed cell with very primitive furniture, and with the filthiest piece of straw matting that I ever saw, until, on a subsequent visit to Calcutta, I had room number "77," in which was a still worse specimen. I picked my way about on both of them, much as a lady crosses a muddy street.

Summoning our Indian servant, we asked him to unpack the sheets, wadded quilts, pillow-cases, and towels which every traveler who respects himself will carry with him through the Indian Empire; but, on turning to inspect my bed, I found that two black crows were perched upon it, like Poe's raven on the "bust of Pallas, just above my chamber door." Apparently, too, they were determined to leave it "nevermore;" for they were as tenacious of their temporary home as Irish peasants resisting an eviction. When they had finally flown away through an open window, I requested that the solitary piece of linen which adorned the couch be removed. Presently, hearing a cooing noise, I looked up toward the ceiling and saw a nest of pigeons in a hole in the wall. Dirt and straw had fallen from this upon my coat

THE GREAT EASTERN HOTEL.

hanging on a chair beneath; and an indifferent servant, summoned in hot haste, at length deliberately climbed a ladder, removed the nest, and stuffed the hole with a newspaper! Such was my room in the best hotel in the capital of England's Indian Empire.

NATIVE LIFE.

On entering the dining-room of the Great Eastern, we found that behind the chair of each guest stood his private servant or "boy." The sight of these bare-footed, white-robed Hindus running about in quest of food, suggested to me a panic-stricken crowd of colored people rushing from their beds at night. When coffee was served at dinner, we could at first obtain no sugar with it, for sugar is not served in bowls upon the table, lest the famished natives empty it into their pockets. A little of it is brought in a wine-glass to each guest, who is also allowed but one spoon. As each servant is responsible for his master's spoon, I saw my attendant, between each course, wipe mine on a napkin when he thought he was observed — otherwise, on his clothing! Even then, there were not spoons enough to go around, and we amused ourselves by watching three or four Hindus struggle for one, and we made bets as to which would carry off the prize.

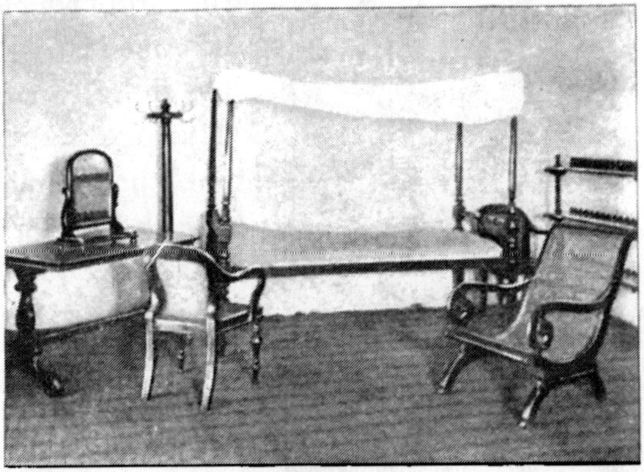

"NO. 54."

THE POST-OFFICE, CALCUTTA.

Where the imposing Post-office of Calcutta now stands took place, in 1756, the tragedy of the "Black Hole of Calcutta." The prison itself, known as the

A MOUNTAIN SANITARIUM, NORTH OF CALCUTTA.

"Black Hole," together with the fort of which it formed a part, has long since disappeared; but throughout the English-speaking world, its name is still suggestive of atrocious cruelty. When the fortress of Calcutta was captured from the English by the Indian prince, Suraj-al-Dowlah, and a horde of natives, the survivors of the garrison, numbering one hundred and forty-six men, were locked up for the night in a room only eighteen feet square and containing but one small window. It was the month of June, when in Calcutta the heat is, under the most favorable circumstances, almost unendurable for Europeans. In vain the suffer-

RELIGIOUS ABLUTION.

ers, who were crowded so closely together that they could scarcely move, implored their jailers to release them, promising them any amount of money in return for liberty. The natives, jeering at their anguish, remained obdurate, and when the dawn revealed the terrible result of those long hours of maddening heat, intolerable thirst, and slow asphyxiation,

THE KING OF BEASTS IN INDIA.

one hundred and twenty-three were dead, and twenty-three pale, haggard men stood raving with delirium or faintly gasping at the window, standing, as on a mound, upon the corpses of their comrades.

One of our first walks in Calcutta was to the river Hugli, in whose waters a multitude of Hindus were bathing, much as we had seen them at Benares. Here, as there, bathing is a religious duty, and prayers are uttered after each

A RETIRED THUG.

ablution. On the bank were many individuals who had been brought here to die; for this river, being one of the mouths of the Ganges, is sacred, and to expire here insures one's entrance into heaven. I was astonished and saddened to find that many of the disgusting features of Hindu idolatry and superstition are as prevalent in Calcutta as in the cities of the interior. We visited, for example, close by the river, a Hindu temple, known as Kalighat, and there beheld more loathsome sights than any which we had witnessed at Benares. The Goddess Kali, who is worshiped here by hundreds of thousands of people yearly, is represented by a hideous idol, with human skulls around her neck and with a mouth apparently reeking with clots of blood. A draught of warm human blood is believed to make her happy for a thousand years. Here in a courtyard, slippery with gore, we saw a sacrifice of kids and goats which are slain every day to appease the

KALIGHAT.

deity. The victims' heads lay about the altar like croquet balls round a finishing stake, and priests, degraded in appearance, offered for a fee to make more sacrifices merely as a spectacle. It should be remembered that this is not an obscure and unimportant temple of Calcutta: on the contrary, it is the most popular Hindu shrine in the city, and the very name Calcutta is derived from Kalighat.

A GROUP OF HINDUS.

Moreover, the goddess Kali was the special patroness of the Thugs, the professional stranglers of India, who for many years committed murders here in the name of religion. These fanatical assassins used to roam about the country in bands of from ten to two hundred. Each man had a special duty to perform; one was the leader; others were scouts; some were pick-bearers; others were grave-diggers. Disguised as pilgrims or merchants, they would associate themselves with their intended victims in the most friendly style until a favorable opportunity presented itself. Then they would suddenly seize and strangle the doomed men, and hide their bodies in graves dug with pickaxes which had been previously blessed by the priests, and were symbolical of the teeth of Kali. Two-thirds of the booty thus obtained was divided among the murderers, and the remainder given to the goddess. Even now, although the British Government has suppressed the Thugs, the Temple of Kali is as popular as ever, and hundreds of thousands still worship at her shrine.

Within the precincts of this temple we beheld several specimens of Indian fakirs, each of whom seemed a combination of beggar, fanatic, impostor, and political spy. In a disgusting area, resembling a garbage heap, a score of these men were seated, entirely naked, upon a mound of ashes, in which they rolled repeatedly. Not content with the results thus gained, they even rubbed the dirt all over their bodies, which had been previously greased in order to retain it. Their hair, matted with filth, reached nearly to their waists, and was painted yellow, and on this they threw occasional handfuls of dust and ashes. Yet when a few of them followed us into the street asking for money, they seemed to attract no attention, although they ran along beside our horse-car, in which were several European women and children. A sickening feeling, similar to that which I had felt in Canton, came over me at the sight of this human degradation; especially when I remembered that there are in India more than a million of

A FAKIR.

THE TAJ FROM THE GARDEN

these half-crazed mendicants and frauds, who are revered and almost worshiped by multitudes of men and women, who will actually stoop and kiss their feet.

It is no wonder, therefore, that after such experiences, forgetful for a moment of the agreeable features of India, the following lines were, in an hour of reaction, inscribed in the author's diary:

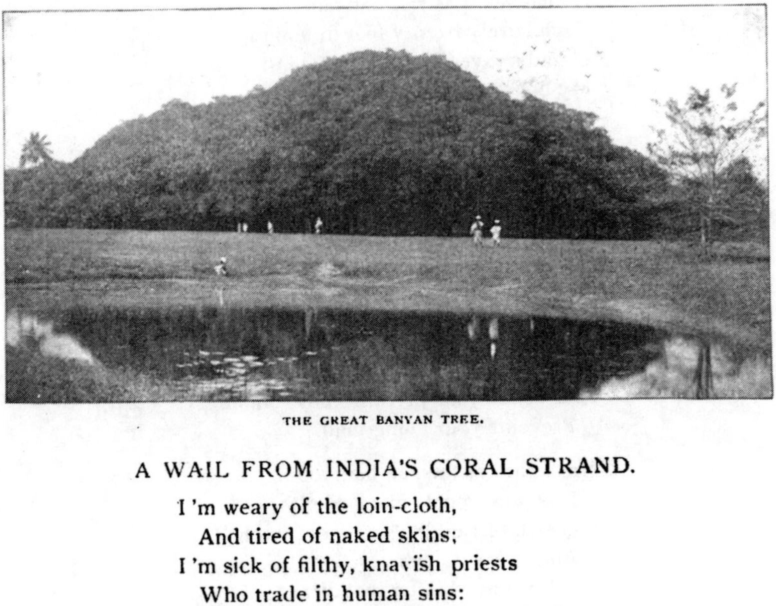

THE GREAT BANYAN TREE.

A WAIL FROM INDIA'S CORAL STRAND.

I 'm weary of the loin-cloth,
  And tired of naked skins;
I 'm sick of filthy, knavish priests
  Who trade in human sins:
These millions of the great unwashed
  Offend both eye and nose;
I long for legs in pantaloons
  And feet concealed in hose.

A wail of human misery
  Is ringing in my ears;
The sight of utter wretchedness
  Has filled my eyes with tears;
The myriad huts of mud and straw
  Where millions toil and die
Are blots upon this fertile land
  Beneath an Orient sky.

I 'm weary of the nasal rings
  And juice-discolored lips;
I cannot bear these brown-skinned brats
  Astride their mothers' hips;
I loathe the spindling Hindu shanks
  With dirt encrusted hard;
I 'm nauseated by the hair
  That reeks of rancid lard.

I 'll ride no more in little cabs
  That serve as railroad-cars,
Each barely twenty feet in length
  And swayed by countless jars;
My bones are racked by traveling
  In India's jerky way:
Far better weeks in Pullman cars
  Than one night in Cathay!

I 'm sick at heart (and stomach too)
  Of India's vile hotels,
Whose rooms are drearier and less clean
  Than many prison cells;
Where servants swarm like cockroaches
  Yet nothing can be had,
And where your private "boy" alone
  Prevents your going mad.

I 'm weary of the sun-hats too
  Like toad-stools made of pith;
I 'm sick of Buddha's "sacred tooth"
  And every other myth.
Good-bye to whining mendicants
  Who show their loathsome sores!—
I 'm glad to take the steamer now,
  And sail for other shores.

It was with great relief that we left Kalighat and its horrors, and made our way to the Botanical Garden, in the suburbs of Calcutta, to view its celebrated banyan tree, the largest in the world. Who can forget this marvelous phenomenon, which furnished one of the illustrations in our school-books twenty-five years ago? It looked larger than I expected; though I should have remembered that it is steadily increasing, year by year, for its vitality seems to rival that of the earth itself. The circumference of its outer tendrils now sweeps through a circuit of one thousand feet!

A YOUNG BANYAN.

Not without awe did we approach and stand beneath its mighty roof. Though the main trunk is fifty feet in circumference, it was not that which most astonished me. What filled me with amazement was its horizontal branches, stretching out on every side for more than one hundred and fifty feet. These drop to the ground hundreds of tiny filaments, which, taking root, become themselves subordinate trees, send up nourishment to the parent stock, hold up its sturdy limbs, and allow them to advance till they can let fall other grappling-irons to the earth and put forth new leaves to the sun. We walked beneath this banyan tree as in a grove, and, sitting within its shade on benches placed for weary travelers, admired this marvelous growth, which, nevertheless, seems here so natural and easy that we involuntarily asked ourselves why other trees do not adopt this

GOING TO CREMATION.

system of indefinite expansion,—this secret of arboreal immortality.

As we were returning from the Botanical Garden, we met two natives carrying, in a kind of sling suspended from a pole, the body of a man.

"Where are they taking him?" I asked.

"To the river Hugli," was the reply.

"Is he dead?"

"Not yet; but he will die soon, and they are anxious that he may expire beside the sacred stream."

"What will become of his body then?"

"It will be cremated at the Burning Ghat."

"Let us go thither!" I exclaimed.

On reaching it, we were introduced to its Hindu superintendent, who is appointed by the English Government to examine all bodies brought there, to ascertain the cause of death and to inform the police if he has reason to suspect a murder. Cremation is one of the characteristic features, not only of Calcutta, but of the whole of India, and in such an overpopulated and unhealthy land it is almost a necessity. What I object to, therefore, is not the act itself, but the coarse, brutal way in which it is usually performed.

UNDER THE BANYAN TREE.

The enclosure of the Burning Ghat is an ill-kept, dirty

area, bounded on one side by a grimy portico. In this we stood to watch the ceremonies. At one end was a kind of cattle-pen, where mourners wait until a vacant space for burning can be given them. I think I can say without much exaggeration that any respectable dog would, after taking one look at that waiting-room, have walked out immediately.

IN THE BURNING GHAT.

Three coolies, whose oily skin glistened in the sun, at length brought in a body on a bamboo litter. This they let fall upon the ground with the same care that an American "baggage-smasher" shows in handling a trunk. By walking ten feet farther, they could, at least, have laid it in the shade: instead of that they left it in the broiling sun. The superintendent asked some questions, and then informed us that the corpse was that of a man who had died half an hour before of rheumatism.

We did not have to wait long for the cremation. Without delay the coolies brought in ten or a dozen logs of wood about four feet in length, and threw them down close to the body. So roughly was this done that some of the sticks bounded six inches from the ground, and I fully expected to see them strike the corpse. Wood is the most expensive factor in this system of cremation. A funeral with the amount of kindling here described costs a dollar; children half-price. Yet even this is not the cheapest method. Sometimes less wood is used. In such cases the body is not entirely consumed, and the remnants must be buried. Formerly they were thrown into the river among the bathers, but this is now prohibited. The funeral-pyre, when constructed, formed a pile of logs, arranged in cross-tiers.

WAITING FOR WOOD.

On this the body was laid, its only covering being a bit of cotton. I could see plainly that the limbs were not yet rigid, nor had the eyes been closed. To make up for the shortness of the pyre the legs were bent back at the knees. Another layer of sticks was then placed upon the body to keep it in position. All was now ready for the burning. It is the Hindu custom for the nearest male relative to light the fire, and in this instance a son of the deceased, about sixteen years of age, took up some wisps of straw, and aided by his little brother six years old, walked around the pile of wood, lighting the kindling on every side. This was not done, however, with solemnity or the least emotion. The other relatives looked on as listlessly as if they were

READY TO LIGHT THE PYRE.

ENGLAND AND INDIA.

assisting at a bonfire, and called out to the son to light it better here or there. A priest was meanwhile mumbling over something like a prayer, but no one paid him the least attention, and two of the body-bearers laughed and talked so boisterously as to drown his voice. "Are the bodies of wealthy Hindus burned in this filthy area?" I inquired.

"Yes," was the reply: "but their pyres usually contain more or less sandal-wood and spices, and large fees are then demanded by the assistants."

ARRANGING THE BODY.

I have dwelt thus on the Hindu system of cremation, not only because it made upon me a profound impression, but also from the fact that it is typical of what is going on all over India. Thousands are burned somewhere in these densely populated provinces every day, and nothing is more strikingly illustrative of Hindu customs. But, as performed here, cremation lacks all delicacy and solemnity, and the last crematory act that I beheld was as revolting as the first.

One of the most remarkable and interesting cities of India

DELHI.

is Delhi. In point of age it challenges comparison with Benares. It antedates by many centuries the Rome of Romulus. It is poetically called the "Rome of Asia." It has been seven times ruined and rebuilt. The desolate plain surrounding it resembles the Campagna. Throughout an area of twenty-four square miles are strewn the fragments of the city's former grandeur. Much of its past is too indefinite to appeal to us; but there is one magnificent epoch in its history, only three hundred years ago, which gives to it a fascination rarely equaled even in the Orient. For Delhi was the capital of India's Mohammedan conquerors,—the favorite home

A RUIN NEAR DELHI.

of those incomparably rich and lavish sovereigns, the Great Moguls.

Perhaps the reader may here knit his brow and say below his breath, "Who were the Great Moguls?" For, owing to the busy lives that we have led since leaving school and college, we possibly remember of them now only what Thomas Moore told us in his poem "Lalla Rookh." Few things are easier to remember, however, than an outline of the Mogul Empire. Only three great heroes in that dynasty need to be recalled,—Baber, the Founder; Akbar, the Ruler; and Shah Jehan, the Builder. No matter for the others. These names are like the three stars in Orion's belt. Who, save astronomers, ever care to trace the rest of that great constellation in the vault of night? Baber, who was born almost contemporaneously with the discovery of America by Columbus, invaded and conquered a large part of India in 1525. His throne was the saddle, his canopy the sky. He was a Mohammedan,—a true specimen of those followers of the Prophet who had already built the Mosque of Cordova in Spain, wrested from Christian hands the sepulchre of Jesus, and placed the crescent on the dome of Santa Sophia

AN ANCIENT FORTRESS.

in Stamboul. He would have been remarkable in any age, for with the talents of a warrior and administrator he combined fondness for literature, music, and architecture. He even wrote his own biography in memoirs which have recently been translated into English. They are extremely interesting,

THE MAUSOLEUM OF AKBAR.

for in them Baber tells without restraint the secrets of his heart. The grandson of this conqueror was Akbar, one of the most successful men that ever occupied a throne. A study of his life astonished me. His was the task not merely to extend his Indian Empire, but to unite the various nationalities of which it was composed. This he accomplished grandly, and, though he was a contemporary of Queen Elizabeth and Henry IV, the romantic story of his victories, his statesmanship, and private life, reads like the history of Julius Cæsar. He was a handsome man, famed for his physical

TOMB OF AKBAR, AGRA.

strength and captivating manners. He was affectionate and loyal to his friends, and ready to forgive his enemies; yet was a most successful warrior and a determined ruler. His breadth of mind was extraordinary. Although born and bred a Moslem, he nevertheless employed, without distinction, both Hindus and Mohammedans, and had among his friends the followers of Brahma, Buddha, Zoroaster, and Jesus. His motto was: "There is good in every creed. Let us adopt what is good and discard the remainder."

When he was dead, men realized with astonishment that during his long reign of forty-nine years India had been exempt from foreign invasions, that universal peace had been established, and that the men of every sect had lived and worshiped in security.

OLD INDIAN SHRINES.

The tomb of Akbar, fifteen miles from Agra, is a noble edifice of richly-tinted sandstone and white marble, combining beauty, strength, and majesty. This was, in fact, the style of architecture that Akbar loved. For, in addition to all else, this emperor built the most imposing structures to be found in India. Not the most beautiful structures: that was the work of Shah Jehan, the builder of the Taj

Mahal. The warlike Akbar built gigantic fortresses. His grandson reared within them the most elaborate palaces this earth has seen. One worked in granite, the other in alabaster;— the genius of the first was akin to that of Michelangelo; that of the second possessed the inspiration of a Raphael.

ONE OF THE APPROACHES TO AKBAR'S MAUSOLEUM.

On the fifth and loftiest story of this mausoleum stands the cenotaph of Akbar, his body being as usual buried in the crypt below. This upper story is a courtyard of white marble. In the centre (its only canopy the sapphire sky) is a sarcophagus of alabaster, richly carved and bearing an appropriate epitaph. Three feet from this rises a marble pedestal, in the top of which is a slight cavity. It gave me an idea of the magnificence of those old days that I had never grasped before, to learn that here, so far above the usual sight of men, once rested that most famous jewel in the world,— the Kohinoor diamond; now in the possession of one, who, though she has never set foot in India, is, nevertheless, the present Empress of the Mogul Empire — Queen Victoria.

To appreciate the third great monarch of the Mogul

Empire, Shah Jehan, one must inspect the palace built by him at Delhi. When I first stepped within the audience-chamber of the Grand Moguls, it seemed to me that all I had read and heard of it had given me no idea of its amazing richness. It so exceeded all my expectations that the result was just the same as if I had not known that such enchanting dreams of Eastern architects had ever been materialized in stone. Here are long corridors and rooms which are not merely paved, roofed, and lined with purest marble; that marble itself is covered with sculptures in relief until each block becomes a masterpiece of art. Nor is this all, for, spreading over the pavement, twined about the columns, and sparkling on the ceilings, are variously colored vines, leaves, and flowers. "Are these walls painted, then?" one naturally inquires. Far from it. This decoration is obtained by means of precious stones, inlaid like Florentine mosaic. Yes, in this palace there are miles of garlands, wreaths, and tendrils, growing apparently in great luxuriance, yet actually composed of jasper, agate, onyx, goldstone, and carnelian, with here and there inscriptions from the Koran, all outlined in mosaic on a background as white as snow.

THE CENOTAPH.

Set in the walls are graceful pockets, such as we see in

the courts of the Alhambra, in which the veiled and jeweled ladies of the palace kept their slippers or their gems. Here in the softened light I could have easily fancied that my outstretched hand might pluck bouquets of roses and camellias. But in reality, the trellises on which they grew were marble screens, and the green leaves and ruby petals of the flowers on these walls glowed in precious stones.

THE MOGUL PALACE AT DELHI.

No words are adequate to portray this sculptured loveliness. Hence, let me ask you to assist me. You have, perhaps a piece of Florentine mosaic which you treasure as a brooch or paper-weight. Expand that into a panel set in an alabaster wall, or into a stately column brilliant as a prism. In your home there is, perhaps, a Persian rug whose colors you admire. Transform that into a mosaic, and with it pave the floor or decorate the roof. Again, you have a bit of Chinese ivory elaborately carved. Magnify that till it forms a mile of marble balustrades. Now multiply these panels, prisms,

PEARL MOSQUE.

JEWELED WALLS.

rugs, and screens and having made of them a fairy palace, delicate as frost-work, insert within its walls a million glittering gems; then, as you gaze enraptured at your workmanship, murmur to yourself, "This is a little like the palace of the Grand Moguls!" Yet what once existed here was vastly richer and more elegant than what is visible to-day. We saw, for example, the corner of an alabaster pedestal,—all that is left now of the famous "Peacock Throne," on which the Mogul emperor sat in majesty. That throne was one of the marvels of the world. It was made by order of Shah Jehan, whose jewelers labored for seven years

FLOWERS IN PRECIOUS STONES.

in its decoration. Its value was no less than thirty million dollars. Its framework was of solid gold, encrusted with innumerable precious stones. Above it stretched a golden canopy fringed with pearls. The back was made to represent two jeweled peacocks with expanded tails, whose colors were reproduced by means of rubies, sapphires, emeralds, and diamonds; while, to crown all, upon the top of this imperial seat was perched a parrot carved from a single emerald.

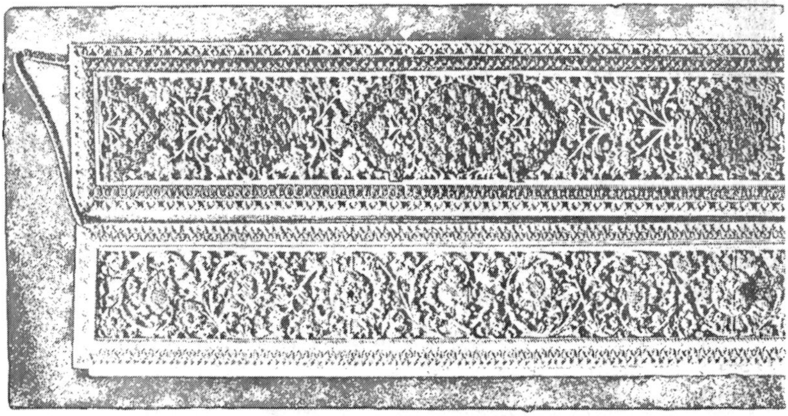

AN IVORY MANUSCRIPT-HOLDER.

We cannot wonder, therefore, that upon these walls was traced in exquisite mosaic a Persian verse whose meaning is as follows:—

"If there be a paradise on earth, it is here."

One is, of course, reminded by this of Moore's rendition of it in his poem, "Lalla Rookh," when he causes one of the inmates of this palace to sing:—

"Come hither, come hither—by night and by day
We linger in pleasures that never are gone;
Like the waves of the summer, as one dies away
Another as sweet and as shining comes on.
And the love that is o'er, in expiring, gives birth
To a new one as warm, as unequall'd in bliss;
And oh! if there be an Elysium on earth,
It is this, it is this."

PEDESTAL OF THE PEACOCK THRONE.

But, alas! there is no Elysium on earth. This certainly was far from being one. Even its builder, Shah Jehan (dethroned by his ungrateful son), was not allowed to occupy it; and after he, the last of the illustrious three, was gone, the end was near. Sooner or later, fate invariably scatters accumulated wealth. The very richness of this Mogul capital attracted the despoiler. Tempted by such a dazzling prize, in 1738, a Shah of Persia captured Delhi and its contents, plundered this gorgeous edifice, and carried off to Teheran the Peacock Throne and more than a thousand camel-loads of gems and precious ornaments, valued, it is said, at four hundred million dollars.

PAST AND PRESENT.

Thirty years ago, after the Indian mutiny, the last of the Moguls, heir to the throne of Akbar and Shah Jehan, was tried by English officers in this

TRAVELING AS FREIGHT.

glorious palace of his ancestors for treason to Great Britain. Judgment was found against him, and, having been banished forever from India, he died a few years later in the British settlement of Burma. Ironical indeed, therefore, seems the inscription on these glittering walls. The Mogul dynasty is gone forever, and in these voiceless corridors of vanished Oriental splendor our echoing footsteps seemed to murmur sadly, "*Sic transit gloria mundi.*"

The morning after our visit to the Mogul palace, we drove far out upon the plain surrounding Delhi. The object of this expedition was to behold a minaret built in honor of the Moslem general, Kutub, who conquered Delhi seven hundred years ago. It is called after him the Kutub Minar. I gazed

IN THE DAYS OF THE MOGULS.

SARCOPHAGUS OF A NATIVE RULER.

upon it with astonishment. Its color was what first impressed me. It is a beautiful Pompeian red, the material being Indian sandstone. Yet, near the top, with exquisite effect, it wears a circle of white marble, like a coronet of pearls, the two combining with the sky to make the glorious tricolor we see so frequently in India—the red, white, and blue. The entire column is fluted from top to bottom, and to relieve it of monotony, it is divided into five sections, marked by projecting galleries of the finest sculpture, so delicately carved that they may be compared to bracelets on a lady's arm. So solidly was this stupendous tower constructed, that not only are its ornamentations still perfect, but not the least crack in its masonry can be discovered, inside or out, despite the lapse of seven hundred years. Some think this to have been a monument of victory rather than a minaret, but it may well have answered both these purposes. At all events, it is the most imposing emblem of Mohammedan power that this earth can show. With the exception of the Washington obelisk, it is the tallest isolated monument in the world. Utterly distinct from any building, this splendid shaft shoots upward to the height of two hundred and fifty feet, tapering gradually all the way, till from a circuit of one hundred and fifty feet at the base, it holds against the sky a ring but ten feet in diameter. Moreover, beautifully carved upon its surface are decorations which may

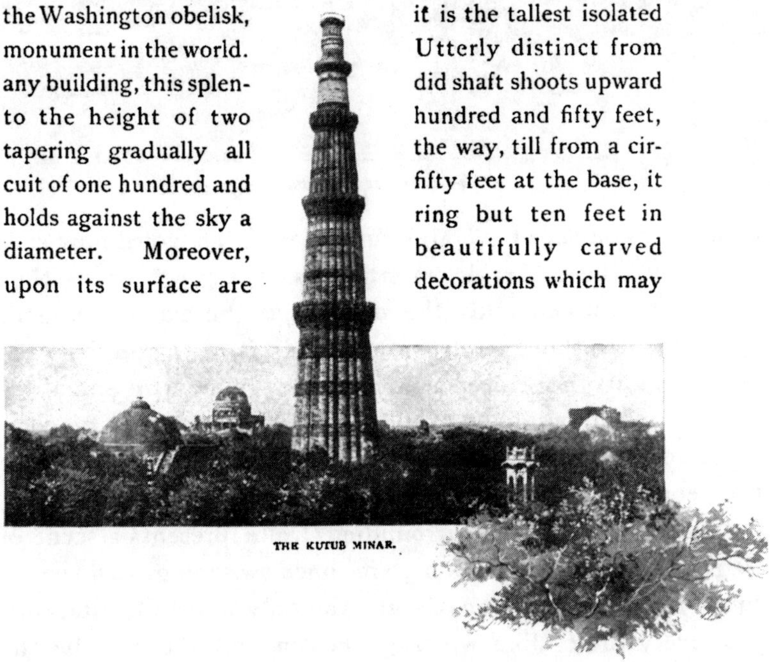

THE KUTUB MINAR.

be compared to sculptured rings. They are broad bands of letters cut into the solid stone, and reproduce in well-nigh indestructible form passages from the Koran. One of them reads as follows: "Allah invites to Paradise and brings into the way of righteousness all who are willing to enter." Unutterably solemn, therefore, seems this mighty column, looking majestically down from its imposing height upon the silent desolation of the plain. For though from

EUROPEAN RESIDENCES.

this, the grandest of all Moslem minarets, no voice now calls to prayer, these Arabic inscriptions still proclaim, as they have done for centuries, the mercy and the majesty of God. As I turned thoughtfully away from it, I could but ask myself: "If the Europeans were to relinquish India to-morrow, what buildings would they leave worthy to be compared for a moment either with this glorious minaret or with the peerless structures of the Great Moguls?"

By night the plain surrounding Delhi presents a scene of singular desolation. Upon a site once swarming with tumultuous life, a few poor hovels are the only human habitations. Yet everywhere, like wreckage floating on the sea, lie the memorials of former greatness. Dilapidated walls, deserted fortresses, ruined mosques, solitary gateways, and crumbling towers are constantly in sight, some still retaining vestiges of strength, others long since reduced to masses of débris. One of these structures is of extraordinary beauty. It is the oldest Moslem tomb known to exist in India, and certainly there are few so richly decorated. The roof, indeed, is gone, and the sarcophagus of alabaster which it protected is now unsheltered from the sun and rain; but the old walls remain intact, and in their frost-like tracery in stone

ONE OF THE KUTUB MINAR'S RINGS.

EXQUISITE STONE TRACERY NEAR DELHI.

remind one of the enchanting work of the Alhambra. Similar tombs are scattered broadcast on this plain; yet what do we really know of any of the kings and warriors buried in them? A feeling of profound sadness took possession of me here, and I recalled the appropriate verses of the Persian poet, Omar Khayyam, written a hundred years before the Kutub Minar arose above this plain.

TRAVELING WITH ELEPHANTS.

"Strange, is it not? that of the myriads who
Before us pass'd the door of Darkness through,
Not one returns to tell us of the Road,
Which to discover we must travel too.

"Think, in this batter'd Caravanserai
Whose Portals are alternate Night and Day,
How Sultán after Sultán with his Pomp
Abode his destin'd Hour, and went his way.

"When You and I behind the Veil are past,
Oh, but the long, long while the World shall last,
Which of our Coming and Departure heeds
As the Sea's self should heed a pebble-cast.

MONUMENT AT CAWNPORE.

"Ah, my Belovèd, fill the Cup that clears
TO-DAY of past Regret and future Fears:
To-morrow!—Why To-morrow I may be
Myself with Yesterday's Sev'n thousand Years.

"Yet Ah, that Spring should vanish with the Rose!
That Youth's sweet-scented manuscript should close!
The Nightingale that in the branches sang,
Ah whence, and whither flown again, who knows!"

The name of Delhi is forever associated with the great Indian mutiny in 1857, when England was suddenly confronted by a revolt of more than one hundred thousand trained Sepoys, or native soldiers, whom she had enrolled, as she supposed, for her defense. A spirit of discontent and hatred of the English had long been latent throughout India, but the immediate cause of the uprising was, as usual in all Indian troubles, a religious one. Cartridges had been given to the troops, and these, it was reported, were greased with lard or tallow, to bite into which (as soldiers were then obliged to do) was to the Hindus a contamination worse than death. The rumor of this sacrilege spread like wild-fire, and regiment after regiment murdered its English officers and

OLD MOSLEM TOMB NEAR DELHI.

turned against the Europeans the weapons they had been taught to use. One part of Delhi is revered by every lover of brave men and valiant deeds. It is the grave of General Nicholson, the hero of the siege of the city in 1857. The superbly built fortress of the Mogul emperors was then held by sixty thousand well-armed natives, many of whom had been soldiers of the British army. Nevertheless, an English force of only seven thousand men, led by the gallant Nicholson, resolved to dislodge them. To do this it was necessary to make an entrance through a structure called the Cashmere

SITE OF THE OLD MOAT.

THE CASHMERE GATE, DELHI.

Gate. This Nicholson ordered to be blown up. It was a desperate undertaking, for it was then surrounded with a moat; but four intrepid heroes volunteered to attempt it. With heavy bags of powder on their heads, they dashed across the moat. The foremost was shot dead; the second fell to rise no more; the third reached the gate and laid the powder, but was wounded; the fourth, however, lighted the train and sprang into the ditch. A moment later there was a fearful explosion,

THE RESIDENCY, LUCKNOW.

the ponderous gate was shattered, and the English troops rushed in to victory and—in the case of Nicholson—to death.

This memorial of British valor was still fresh in our minds when, shortly after leaving Delhi, we reached Lucknow and stood within its former Residency. It is now a ruin, deeply scarred by shot and shell; but vines and flowers do their best to hide the ravages of cruelty and strife, and its old walls possess a serene and melancholy beauty peculiarly their own. Here, at the time of the mutiny, the position was exactly the reverse of that at Delhi. In this case, the English were the besieged. Scantily protected by these walls, through five long months of Indian summer heat, a force of about sixteen hundred fighting men, encumbered by five hundred women and children, heroically kept at bay no less than fifty thousand natives, who were not ignorant savages with uncouth instruments of war, but well-armed native soldiers, trained by British officers.

THE OLD WALLS AT LUCKNOW.

Passing beyond the Baillie gate, through which at last, after those awful months of siege, the rescuing army forced its way, we saw the room where the commander of that garrison, the lion-hearted Henry Lawrence, when mortally wounded by a shell, received the sacrament and breathed his last. He was almost the only man in India who had foreseen the coming storm in time to store up ammunition and prepare for war. As a rule, the mutiny took the British by surprise. So thoroughly had they relied upon their native regiments, that many British troops had been called home for the Crimean War. Only about twenty thousand English soldiers had been left in India, and these were scattered over an enormous territory, with scarcely any railroads to facili-

SNAKE-CHARMERS.

tate their concentration. One can but marvel, therefore, that any foreigners were left to tell the tale. But English steadfastness and valor proved too much for even those appalling odds, and India was saved to England by just such heroes as Sir Henry Lawrence, who, as his life blood ebbed away, whispered the words inscribed upon his tomb: "I have tried to do my duty. May the Lord have mercy on my soul."

THE BAILLIE GATE, LUCKNOW.

When the remains of this noble patriot and Christian were laid to rest, the fighting was so severe that none of his officers dared to leave his post. But, one by one, the soldiers who bore him to the grave, ere they lowered him into the earth, lifted the sheet which covered the face of their beloved commander, and reverently kissed his brow.

Still bearing in mind those fearful days of '57, we journeyed from Lucknow to the town of Cawnpore. Tranquil enough it seems to-day, yet, forty years ago, there was enacted here one of the most awful tragedies ever recorded on the page of history. There was no fort in Cawnpore, and, accordingly, when the mutiny broke out, the old commander, Sir Hugh Wheeler, assembled all the European residents in an open field, and raised around them a low wall of earth. To defend this position he could only muster about four hundred English soldiers, more than seventy of whom were invalids. Opposed to them were three thousand Sepoys, armed with muskets and cannon. Moreover, into this unsheltered area the dreadful sun of India poured all day long its burning rays, almost as deadly in their effect as shot and shell. Making our way across this ground — mute witness of that physical and mental anguish, —we stood beside the solitary well upon which these poor refugees depended for their water.

ROOM WHERE SIR HENRY LAWRENCE DIED.

To get this precious liquid men had to go at night; for in the day, exposed to a sharp fire from the natives, to venture here meant certain death. The sight of it reminds one that two hundred English ladies, who had never known hardship or discomfort, together with many young and delicate children, were forced to lie, half mad with thirst, behind low earthworks, or else in holes dug in the ground, partially shaded from the deadly sun by garments stretched on the points of bayonets.

After twenty-one days, when Sir Hugh Wheeler had himself fallen ill, and when the wretched garrison was desperate from sickness and starvation, they received a proposition from the native leader, Nana. He solemnly swore by the sacred Ganges that if they would surrender and lay down their arms, he would conduct them safely to the river, half a mile away, and send them all in comfortable boats down to the British colony at Allahabad. It was decided to accept the offer. Accordingly, the next morning, having given up their weapons, all the survivors, including the wounded and the children, left the area where they had endured such misery, and started for the river, along a path where there now stands a fine memorial church erected in their honor. Nana, upon whose promise they were thus relying, cannot be classed with any Zulu chief or

THE FIELD AT CAWNPORE.

THE WELL.

North American Indian. He was a native prince,—the owner of a splendid palace. Some of the ladies then tottering toward the river, more dead than alive, had danced at balls given at his residence. The officers, too, had drunk champagne with him and thought him a most courteous fellow—for an Indian. The reason for Nana's treachery is plain. His father, when dethroned by England like so many other Indian princes, had been richly pensioned. Upon his death, Nana demanded the continuance of the pension. The British Government refused. Thenceforth, beneath that prince's suave and elegant manners lurked a thirst for vengeance. No one suspected him — he was so hospitable, so refined! Even his secretary had been lionized in London, and had

A VILLAGE STREET.

A PRINCESS.

THE MEMORIAL CHURCH.

been sent to the Crimea to study the art of war.

Beside the river is a stairway known as the "Staircase of the Massacre." Down these steps the prisoners made their way with hope and joy. The boats were there. "Surely," they thought, "there is no treachery: Nana has kept his word." While the women and children gladly went on board, on one side of the staircase stood the Englishmen; upon the other, Nana and his officers. Suddenly Nana raised his sword. It was the signal for the butchery. At once a battery, till then concealed, poured on the wretched prisoners a storm of grape-shot. Sir Hugh fell dead at once. Only

THE GRAVE OF MANY HEROES, CAWNPORE.

four wounded men, by feigning death and floating down the stream, succeeded in escaping. The women and children, however — then a company of widows and orphans — were brought on shore, reserved for a more dreadful fate. Filled with unutterable horror, they must have envied then their husbands, fathers, and brothers, who had been killed before their eyes. A beautiful memorial park now occupies the place to which they were conducted.

NEAR THE STEPS OF SLAUGHTER.

Here, for three weeks, in the appalling heat of India in July, two hundred and six European ladies and children were pent up in two stifling rooms. Upon the women the natives inflicted such insults as they liked, for they well knew that nothing would so lacerate English hearts as brutal treatment of their women. But when the troops of General Havelock

THE STAIRCASE OF THE MASSACRE.

were reported to be near, Nana ordered all these prisoners to be brought out and shot. In an agony of dread, the women clung to each other so closely that it was impossible to separate them. Accordingly, the butchers finally rushed in upon them with drawn swords and bayonets, and amid heart-rending shrieks and piteous prayers the deed was done. There is in Cawnpore now a soldier who was one of the army of General Havelock, and who arrived here just four hours after the massacre. He told us that when he first beheld the scene of this slaughter he almost fell to the earth with horror. Upon the walls were traced in blood a few agonized messages to friends at home. There, too, were bullet-marks and sabre-cuts; not high up, as if men had fought with men, but low down and about the corners, where the poor crouching victims had been cut to pieces. Saddest of all, scattered upon the blood-smeared floor, were locks of golden hair and little children's shoes and playthings. The sight of these things drove the English troops to madness, and bearded men who had beheld, unmoved, the horrors of a hundred battles, sat down and wept in sickening anguish; then rose again, steeled evermore against a cry for mercy!

A VETERAN OF HAVELOCK'S ARMY.

In the memorial park, surrounded by a beautifully sculptured screen, is the historic well, whither, on seeing the natives coming toward them, ten English women rushed, and, without hesitation, first threw their children in and then leaped in themselves. Into this abyss the mutilated remains of those who had been massacred were also subsequently thrown, — mothers and children, the dying and the dead in one red, palpitating mass. Above this well, which forms the burial-place of more than two hundred victims, an angel stands in snow-white raiment, so pure, so beautiful, and so pathetic from the memories which it evokes that at the sight the eyes grow dim with tears. One feels that it is "holy ground." The angel's arms are crossed upon the breast in resignation, while in each hand is held the martyr's palm. Over the archway is inscribed: "These are they who came out of great tribulation." Around the well-curb, too, I read these words: "Sacred to the perpetual memory of the great company of Christian people, chiefly women and children, who

FORMER HOME OF NANA.

THE MEMORIAL WELL.

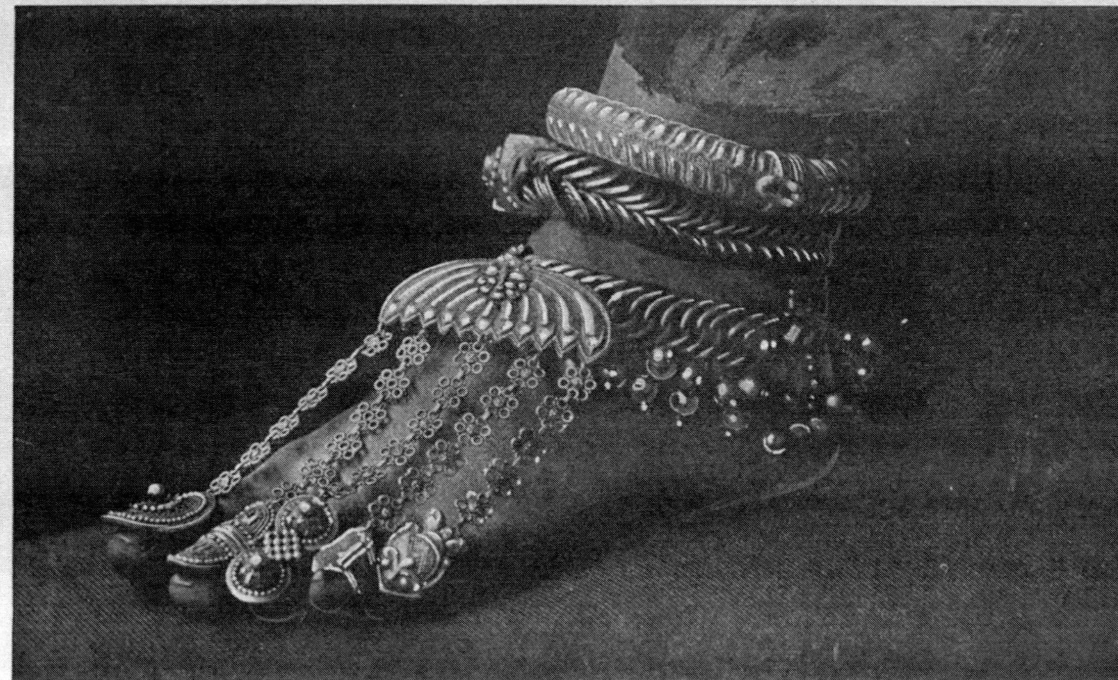

THE FOOT OF A PRINCESS.

near this spot were cruelly massacred by the followers of the rebel Nana, and cast, the dying with the dead, into the well below, on the 15th day of July, 1857."

"No native is allowed to enter this enclosure," said the old soldier who here serves as guardian. We could not wonder at the law.

Leaving this hallowed spot, we drove to a point beside the river Ganges, whence we could see the former residence

AN INDIAN LANDSCAPE.

of Nana,—the wretch upon whose guilty soul rests this inhuman crime. What became of him no one can tell. The British government offered a reward for his arrest, but he was never found. Some think this human tiger perished in the jungle. Others maintain that he is still alive, living in safety in the north of India, beyond the English lines. At all events, his fiendish work is over now, and the historic stream, once stained with England's bravest blood, now flows on peaceful and clear, just as within the lovely garden at the well the air which once resounded to the shrieks of anguish now echoes to the songs of birds.

In addition to the tragedy at Cawnpore, horrible deeds of

cruelty were enacted in other parts of India. In Delhi, delicate ladies and beautiful young girls were stripped of their clothing and driven naked through the streets, stoned, beaten, pelted with offal, and finally given over to the brutal passions of the rabble, until the terrified and horror-stricken women became raving maniacs or sank in death. More than once the fiends snatched children from their mother's arms and dashed their brains out on the walls. Some families, too, are said to have been burned to death. Surely, it is not strange that when the English once more gained the mastery, they blew a number of these demons from the cannon's mouth.

A SOLDIER AND CAMEL.

A few days after leaving Cawnpore, I saw, in company with an English officer, some native regiments on parade. I asked him frankly what he thought about the chances of another mutiny. His answer was a guarded one. "We are more careful now," he said: "our British force will never again be so reduced as it was in '57. It numbered then only 39,000 men as compared with 225,000 native soldiers. Moreover, while we use Indian troops for infantry and cavalry, we keep most of the cannon in our own hands; and do not forget that we have now a system of railways and telegraphs, which means that we can put down any insurrection quickly and effectively." But several civilians with whom we conversed

NATIVE TROOPS.

did not take this optimistic view. According to them, a vast majority of Hindus and Mohammedans would rise to-morrow, if they dared, especially if Russia's guns began to rouse the echoes of the Himalayas. Their first step undoubtedly would be to cut the telegraph wires and destroy the railroads; and how much better off, they ask, would Europeans then be in India? Many a Maharajah is said to be secretly as discontented as was the rebel Nana. These fires of hate are merely smouldering now, but who can say they will not some day burst forth into a flame? At all events, it is significant that no natives, outside the army, are allowed to own or carry firearms.

AN ENGLISH REGIMENT.

It must be remembered also that, although in her schools and universities England is educating thousands of these natives and giving them employment, nevertheless it is just this class that is most discontented. They have learned enough to believe, and even to assert, that the original inhabitants of a country should govern it, and that it is absurd for a handful of Englishmen, whose home is in another portion of the globe, to rule three hundred million people, entirely distinct from them in race, ideas, customs, and religion. Meantime, at the other end of the social scale are millions of fanatics who hate Europeans from religious motives, and would starve to death rather than eat a particle of food which Christian hands had

SOME SUBJECTS OF GREAT BRITAIN.

touched. Between these two opposing forces England stands to-day.

The dwellings of the common peasants on the plains of India suggested to my mind feathered dog-houses, sometimes surmounted by a second story, where the inmates keep a look-out for crows. One readily sees that the vast majority of these people do not understand the character and customs of the men who govern them. The Hindus, for example, living on a little rice, and thinking it an atrocious crime to kill an animal, regard with horror and contempt the godless foreigners who gorge themselves with beef and mutton; and the Mohammedans, who are forbidden by the Koran to touch intoxicating drinks, shudder to see Europeans consume astonishing quantities of brandy, whisky, and champagne. A

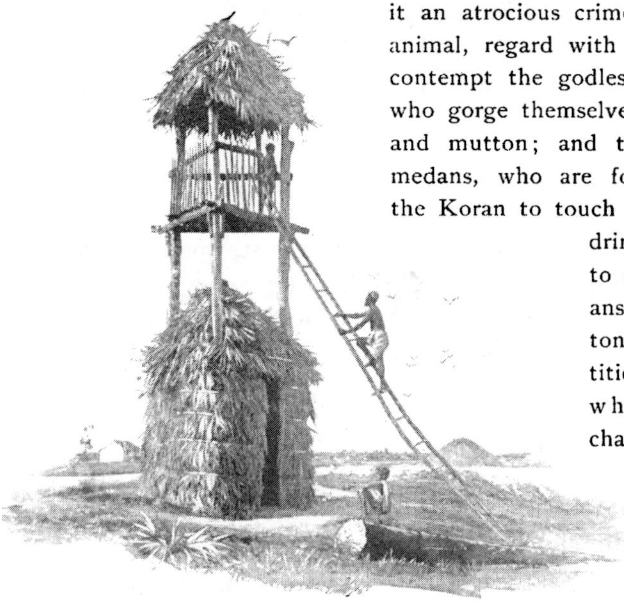

A LOOKOUT FOR CROWS.

AN OPEN-AIR BOUDOIR.

story is told of a Hindu servant who was devotedly attached to his English master. When the latter died, the native desired to carry out the Oriental custom of comforting the spirit of the deceased by bringing to his tomb a sample of the food of which, in life, he had been especially fond. Accordingly, he knelt beside his master's grave, and, with tears

TEA PICKING IN INDIA.

streaming down his cheeks, poured out to the dead Englishman a copious libation of — brandy and soda.

When one occasionally gains a glimpse of one of the Indian princes whom England has deposed, he naturally asks (as they themselves no doubt, have often done), "What right have the English in India, anyway?" About the same right they have in Burma and a score of other places; the same right that the French possess in Siam, or that various nations now have in the continent of Africa. The recent

AN INDIAN PRINCE.

history of Oriental politics is, after all, a simple one. Stripped of all glittering rhetoric, the situation is just this: Europe desires to control the trade of a certain country, and sends out merchants to obtain it. If the unfortunate country does not wish to trade, Europe bombards her till she yields and business is established. Of course, complications soon arise. The Orient is always in the wrong. A war ensues. The Orient is defeated and must pay indemnity. In order to collect it, European officers are appointed, and the unhappy country is taken under European "protection," which means, eventually, not only annexation, but the appropriation of much private property. There have been writers, even among the English, bold enough to declare that England had no more right to the private jewels of one of the kings whom she dethroned in India than to the crown diamonds of Russia.

PALACE OF A DETHRONED PRINCE.

Yet, in justice to England, it

should be remembered that, although other European nations feign to regard such conduct with the utmost horror, they are all watching for a chance to do the same thing. The principal difficulty seems to be that England has appropriated almost everything in sight. The other nations, therefore, are in the position of the smaller lions, represented in the picture of Daniel in the lion's den, of which a Sunday-school boy once said to his teacher: "Please, ma'am, those little lions in the corner are n't going to get any Daniel at all!" It should be said, however, that England succeeds in her colonization where other nations often fail; for she invariably sends the trader first, and then the soldier. France, on the contrary, usually sends the soldier first, and hence the trader sometimes does not come at all.

A MAHARAJAH.

An incident in my experience well illustrates these different modes of colonization. In sailing down the coast of China, from Hong-Kong to India, we stopped at the French settlement of Saigon. To our surprise, we were there able to attend an opera given by a company brought direct from

Paris. The French Government, at an expense of twenty-five thousand dollars, had sent it out there for the season, to keep the colonists from being so homesick that they would return to France. "Great Heavens!" cried one of our English passengers, "I wish Gladstone would do that for us. But in our colonies life 'means business' from the start. We young men come out here to succeed, or to go to the wall. It is a case of the survival of the fittest. The mother country practically says to every one of us, as she casts us into the world, 'Root, hog, or die.' "

SAILING SOUTH TO INDIA.

That British occupation is on the whole a blessing to India I have not the slightest doubt. Whether the English really have a right to dominate the Mogul Empire, or not, there can be only one opinion as to the superiority of Anglo-Saxon rule over the usual tyranny of Indian princes. The British Government has built in India railways, bridges, high-roads, churches, hospitals, and schools. It has established national universities. It has abolished many horrible religious customs, such as the burning alive of widows, and death beneath the car of Juggernaut; and, above all, it has given to India courts of justice, in which all natives, rich or poor,

A RELIGIOUS FESTIVAL.

Brahmins or Pariahs, can have their rights defended by the grand old principles of English law.

The city which, more than all the rest of India, delights and satisfies the traveler, lies in the heart of the old Mogul Empire and is known as Agra. It surpasses even Delhi in its magnificent memorials of the Mogul dynasty. Three structures are especially remarkable in this old capital of Akbar: the Mausoleum of the Prince Itmad-ud-Daulat, the Mogul Palace, and the Taj Mahal. It is true, the first of these lies across the river Jumna, at a little distance from the city, and many tourists fail to visit it. But were it not for its proximity to the incomparable Taj, this tomb would be regarded as one of the marvels of India and would

STONE CARVINGS OF AN INDIAN TEMPLE.

AN INDIAN RAILWAY STATION.

of itself repay a lengthy pilgrimage.

Itmad-ud-Daulat was the father-in-law and prime minister of the Mogul emperor, Jahangir, who succeeded his father Akbar in 1605. His mausoleum stands, as is usually the case in India, in a beautiful garden, whose foliage and flowers form a lovely framework for the pure white marble of the edifice. The Oriental architects who worked for the Moguls thoroughly understood the value of perspective and the solemnity and dignity imparted to such structures by a gradual approach on

TOMB OF ITMAD-UD-DAULAT, AGRA.

marble pavements framed in verdure. This building is so perfectly proportioned that it is a constant pleasure to behold it, even from a distance, and when one comes to its threshold and examines it in detail, his admiration is unbounded. For the entire edifice without and within, in its windows, doors, walls, and graceful towers is a masterpiece of carved and per-

A GORGEOUS MAUSOLEUM.

forated marble, inlaid with precious stones. On the outside, the walls are beautiful expanses of the mosaic work called *pietra dura*, arranged in rectangles, diagonals, diamonds, cubes, stars, and other geometrical designs. While the arches are adorned with flowers carved in marble, the inner walls and niches are embellished with flowers in mosaic, whose colors, set in jewels, never fade. In the place of windows also are placed alabaster screens, so exquisitely cut and perforated that they appear like white lace curtains, through whose fine apertures the sunbeams filter to a dust of gold.

This tomb is not a rival of the Taj Mahal. It could not be, for the Taj is the most beautiful structure in the world. But, being smaller, this can perhaps be studied to better advantage, and, since the style of decoration in both build-

THE FORT AT AGRA.

ings is very similar, this can explain some features of the greater edifice, which might, in the confused emotions there awakened, escape our notice. Moreover, the Taj appeals to us as an expression of man's love for woman. This tomb has no such sentiment connected with it, and merely marks the resting-place of one almost unknown to history, and whose very name is spelled in half a dozen ways. Nevertheless, it is one of the most beautifully proportioned and richly decorated buildings in the world; and as I turned at the entrance of the lovely garden to take a farewell view of its enameled walls and jeweled towers, I thought the scene a perfect illustration of the well known lines:

> "A palace lifting to eternal summer
> Its marble halls from out a glossy bower
> Of coolest foliage, musical with birds."

GROUP OF FEMALE TEACHERS.

In Agra as in Delhi, stands a mighty fortress, built by Akbar. I could not think of this as a mere citadel. It seemed rather a city in itself; for it is nearly two miles in circumference, and is entirely enclosed by ramparts seventy feet in height. Around it winds a moat a hundred feet in breadth, from which at frequent intervals rise massive towers, like mediæval castles on the Rhine. The color of this belt of masonry is a deep red, which in the glow of sunset is suggestive of the sanguinary scenes it has so often looked upon. At such a time one easily fancies that the moat itself is filled with blood, whose horrible reflection paints itself upon the stone.

Its massive gateway, guarded constantly by sentinels, is a reminder that the primary object of this structure is defense. At all events, a large amount of arms and ammunition is now stored within its walls; and in the event of another mutiny, this would become invaluable as a place of refuge. In the days of the Mogul emperors this fortress was a kind of strong box, containing the palace and the sacred treasures of the empire. To some extent it is so still. For, though the throne of the Moguls has fallen, and their resplendent diadems and diamond-hilted swords have all passed into other hands,

THE GATEWAY.

yet even now this beautifully sculptured casket holds some architectural jewels that have few equals in the world.

The first of these to greet the tourist as soon as he has passed the portal, is called the Pearl Mosque, and from its spotless purity and beauty it deserves the name; for everywhere in its enclosure,—roof, columns, walls, and pavement are as white as alabaster. No other sanctuary on earth exhibits such simplicity and purity. Here are no images or paintings,

A CORNER OF THE FORT, AGRA.

or even gilding; one is surrounded only by the chaste white marble, with vines and flowers carved upon it in relief. Oh, the immeasurable superiority of this immaculate pearl of Oriental architecture over the sickening idolatry and filth of Hinduism! No furniture, not even a rug, profanes this beautiful expanse; but the marble pavement is carefully divided by the sculptor's chisel into rectangular spaces, on each of which a follower of Mahomet may kneel in prayer. What an example is this of the restraining power of the Mohammedan religion! For, more than twelve hundred years ago, the Koran forbade the followers of the Prophet to make any

EXTERIOR OF THE PEARL MOSQUE.

likeness of animal life, lest it should lead to idolatry; and during all these centuries that rule has been obeyed. The Moslems, it is true, have thus been kept from cultivating painting and sculpture, but what have they not accomplished

THE PEARL MOSQUE.

in architecture, from Granada to Damascus, and from these Mogul palaces to the Taj Mahal!

At a little distance from this mosque, but still within the fort, stands the palace in which the Mogul emperors resided when at Agra. It seems as if the inmates of such glorious halls should have led lives as full of joy as their apartments were of beauty. Yet sculptured stone, however exquisite, can never satisfy the heart, and even jeweled walls cannot

A PAVILION, AGRA.

atone for loss of liberty. So it was here. Its builder was the lavish Shah Jehan, who also built the equally magnificent palace at Delhi and the incomparable Taj Mahal. And yet he spent the last seven years of his life here, a hopeless captive, imprisoned by his rebellious son; experiencing thus that bitterest of sorrows,—ill-treatment and ingratitude from a heartless child. One thing, however, gave Shah Jehan some consolation; for, when all others had abandoned him, his faithful daughter would not leave him. She voluntarily shared his long imprisonment, striving to make her

A MARBLE SCREEN.

TOMB OF JEHANARA.

love atone for all that he had lost. Her very name, "Jehanara," was but the softened echo of his own, and it was in giving birth to this child that the Emperor's idolized wife had died. Renowned for wit and beauty, she might have held a brilliant place at her brother's court; but she preferred the prison of her father, displaying thus the noble traits of character that have immortalized her memory.

Nothing in India is more pathetic than her burial-place. Having seen the hollowness of royal luxury, she begged,

A PORTION OF THE PALACE AT AGRA.

when on her death-bed, that grass and flowers should be her only covering. Her wish has been respected. It is true an alabaster screen now forms a frame-work for her couch of death, but the space thus enclosed is covered merely with green turf. Upon the marble headstone are inscribed these words: "Let no rich canopy adorn my grave. These simple flowers are most appropriate for one who was poor in spirit, though the daughter of Shah Jehan."

THE PRISON OF SHAH JEHAN.

The pavilion in which the Mogul sovereign was imprisoned was, like all the rest of the palace, replete with luxury and beauty; yet its inmate was a broken-hearted man. He had enjoyed unlimited power: it was his no more. He had erected buildings which even to-day astonish and delight the world: this he could do no longer. He had so dearly loved his wife, that when she died he reared for her the fairest mausoleum which this earth has ever seen; yet when it was completed he could not enter it

HIMALAYAN SCENERY.

to weep beside her grave. Worse than all, the man who had thus robbed him of his throne, his wealth, his occupation, and his liberty, besides murdering his three remaining sons, was his own child by the woman he had so adored!

In realizing these facts, one naturally asks: "Was not this Mogul emperor a Mohammedan, and do not Moslems usually regard their wives as pretty toys,—mere creatures of a day,

AUDIENCE HALL AND TERRACE, AGRA.

who have not even souls to insure them immortality?" Undoubtedly; and this, indeed, is the mystery and marvel of it all, that such a man (the sovereign of an Eastern court, with all material pleasures open to his choice) should have so idolized his lawful wife that when she died he vowed to build for her the grandest tomb that man could frame, and kept his promise, too, although the work required twenty years. Yet this woman, who was the joy and light of his life, was no young bride, whose early death had made her seem to him an ideal character. She was the mother of his children; and when at last she died in his arms, he had been wedded to her fourteen years.

We stood with reverence beside the window of his room, and saw in the distance, as he so often did, the peerless monu-

THE ENTRANCE TO THE GARDEN OF THE TAJ.

ment of love he reared to her,—the Taj Mahal. Toward those white domes, whose soft reflection lay like pearls within the adjacent stream, his dying eyes were turned as over them crept the film of death. Within that wonderful edifice he is buried with the one he loved. For, far more merciful in death than he had been in life, his son allowed the body of the deposed emperor to be borne thither to repose beside that wife whom this majestic structure will make famous to the end of time.

Leaving the Mogul palace, we drove along the river to the beautiful park of forty acres that surrounds the Taj. This garden, which is to the Taj what the setting is to the jewel, is entirely enclosed by a lofty wall. Grandeur and beauty here go hand in hand, for the gateway to this area is no less than one hundred and forty feet in height and a hundred feet in breadth, and its red sandstone frame is exquisitely decorated with mosaic in white marble. Impatient, however, to behold a still greater treasure, we passed beneath this portal and gazed upon the Taj itself. It was still distant. Between us and its pure white form we saw a garden of great beauty. Down through the centre led a stately avenue with marble pavement white as snow. Beside it was a canal of water, from which at times a score of fountains rose like silver trees. Within its limpid flood a thousand goldfish gleamed like jewels in the sunlight. On the right and left stood rows of cypress trees, like funeral plumes; while farther still were groves of palms and orange trees, whose foliage is swayed by

LOOKING TOWARD THE TAJ.

breezes fragrant with the breath of flowers. Thousands of roses bloom here during the entire year, sacred to death and to a deathless love. Speechless, as in a dream, we walked on through this flowery paradise, and drew still nearer to the Taj. Letting our gaze move slowly from its base to its summit, two hundred and ninety-six feet, above our heads, we noted, first, a massive platform of red sandstone, measuring on each side a thousand feet. From this a marble terrace rises to serve as a pedestal for the Taj itself. As for the structure in the centre, the first bewildering glance revealed what seemed to be a delicately sculptured mountain of pure alabaster, supporting on its crest a sparkling dome, light as a radiant bubble, which might at any moment float away and vanish into air. After one rapturous look at its sublime proportions the last doubt was dispelled forever. The conquest was complete; and I became a worshiper of the Taj, like all the millions who had gone before me. The fundamental secret of this charm, like that of most things that are truly great, is its simplicity. It is not complicated in design. It has the purity and simple majesty of the Jungfrau. It is to Saracenic, what the Athenian Parthenon was to Grecian art. The mind can grasp it without effort. Its perfect harmony recalls the phrase of Madame de Staël, that "architecture is frozen music." One part balances another, the platform is proportioned to the pedestal, the smaller domes to the great central one, and the minarets to the entire structure. It is the one completely faultless edifice that man

A MOUNTAIN OF ALABASTER.

INDIA'S CORAL STRAND.

has reared. Passing slowly around it, we viewed the Taj from the bank of the river Jumna. At each of the four corners of its pedestal a marble minaret springs heavenward, like a silver arrow, piercing the air one hundred and forty feet above the pavement, and on the eastern as well as on the western side of the huge platform stands a graceful mosque. No doubt these mosques and minarets were deemed essential, lest this majestic edifice should turn men's thoughts from heaven. At all events, from one of these four marble shafts, uplifted toward the sky, there floats out on the air, five times a day, the muezzin's musical reminder of the only God.

GATEWAY SEEN FROM THE GARDEN.

LACEWORK IN MARBLE.

A SECTION OF THE TAJ.

Our admiration of the Taj was still further increased, when we examined its marvelous decorations. Around each archway, inlaid in black marble, are delicate arabesques and countless verses from the Koran,—the graceful Oriental characters mingling and intertwining like the finest scroll-work or the slender stems and tendrils of a creeping vine. The

THE SCREEN OF ALABASTER.

walls appear almost as massive as the eternal hills, yet on their milk-white surface thousands of roses, tulips, hyacinths, and daisies are sculptured in relief, as though real garlands had been hung here once with such consummate skill that some delighted *genie* of the Arabian Nights had, by a stroke of the enchanter's wand, transformed them into stone. As I surveyed them with delight, I caught my breath to think of all the labor represented here, and of the patient fingers (long since turned to dust), which planted all these jeweled flowers in their snow-white beds, and made them bloom unchanged from century to century. The Taj, which was begun in the year 1630, is said to have occupied twenty thousand men for twenty years. All India furnished its materials. The marble came from one province, the sandstone from another. The Punjab sent it jasper; Ceylon gave sapphires and lapis-lazuli; and agate, onyx, turquoises, and carnelians came from Thibet, Persia, and Arabia. A twilight gloom pervades the interior of this wonderful mausoleum; but if electric light could suddenly be introduced here, one could believe himself within Aladdin's cave. For then the walls would show with dazzling effect their inlaid agate, jasper, bloodstone, and carnelian. It seems as if the emperor, in madness at his loss, and counting earthly wealth as nothing, had thrust his arms repeatedly into the glittering coffers of the Mogul treasury, and, drawing forth

A TOWER AT AGRA.

great handfuls of rare gems, had scattered them upon this tomb, as ordinary men would lay upon a grave bouquets of flowers. In the very centre of the mausoleum I saw what seemed to be a circular frame of lace suspended from the roof by unseen cords. It is, in reality, a screen of alabaster, six feet in height and sixty in circumference. Each panel is a single piece of alabaster several inches thick, yet carved

THE TOMBS OF SHAH JEHAN AND HIS WIFE.

with so much elegance and skill that one must touch it to believe it stone. Within this exquisite enclosure are two marble cenotaphs, completely covered with mosaic-work in precious stones, one hundred being sometimes used to represent a single flower; and through this mass of floral decorations runs a delicate Persian script, telling the story of these royal lovers in lines of which each letter is a gem.

Appropriately enough the sweetest echo in the world dwells in this jeweled cavern. The dome receives all sounds within its silvery crucible, transforms them into purest harmony, and sends them down again as if the upper space were tenanted by a celestial choir, chanting an endless requiem to this ideal union both in life and death. It is particularly sensitive to gentle sounds, and a few notes, sung softly here, float up in rhythmic waves to break upon the concave of the marble arch again, and yet again, until they tremblingly die away like whispered accents of impassioned love. Can anything be more beautiful than this—a building dedicated to the memory of a beloved wife, and at the same time the most perfect structure in the world? It is the grandest yet most delicate homage that man has ever paid to womankind.

There are at least two places in this world where moonlight is essential to complete our happiness—they are Venice and Agra. I had arranged the date of my arrival here with this in view, and hence it was my inestimable privilege to stand here at midnight on the thirty-first of December. Then, gazing on this miracle of beauty, I watched the Old Year take its flight and the New Year steal in with noiseless footsteps, as if to pay its first devotions to the Taj. And as I saw the moonlight gild the slender minarets, till they appeared like beautiful wax tapers lighting this abode of death, and then beheld the Taj itself, one glorified expression of immortal genius, it seemed too wonderful to be reality. It was, in truth, a dream in marble, and, sweetest of all dreams—a dream of love.